T0368618

Rosie Maisonave

NUTMEG FLOWERS PRESENTS

FLOWERS

BEAUTIFUL BLOOMS FOR HOME GARDENS

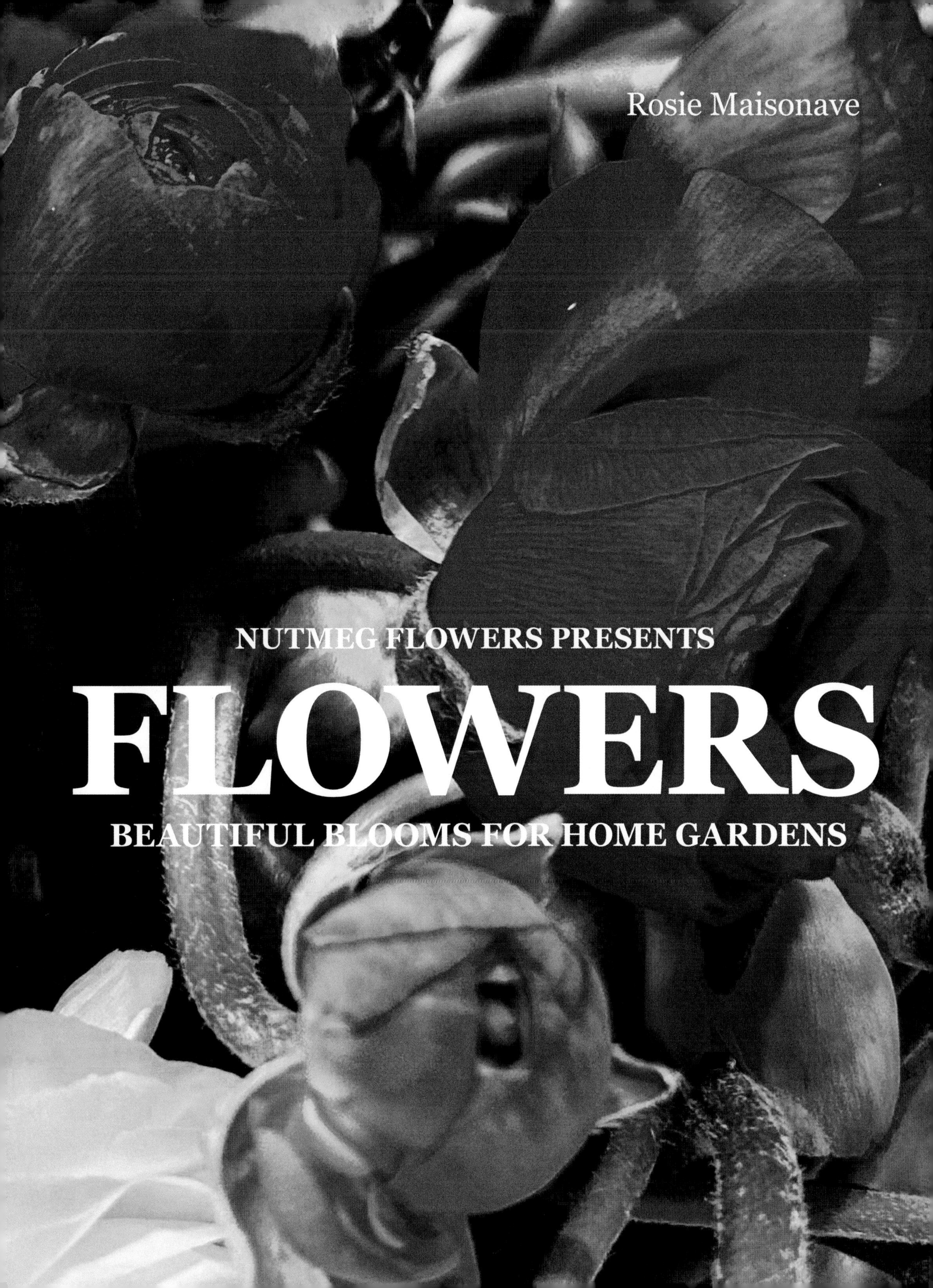

AuthorHouse™
1663 Liberty Drive
Bloomington, IN 47403
www.authorhouse.com
Phone: 833-262-8899

This book is printed on acid-free paper.

ISBN: 979-8-8230-0426-8 (sc)
       979-8-8230-0427-5 (hc)
       979-8-8230-0425-1 (e)

Library of Congress Control Number: 2023905397

Print information available on the last page.

Published by AuthorHouse 06/16/2023

authorHOUSE®

TO MY WONDERFUL HUSBAND
WHO HAS SUPPORTED ME THROUGHOUT THIS
AWESOME ADVENTURE ... I LOVE YOU!

Cover: Photography by Rosie Maisonave
rosie.maisonave@gmail.com
Nutmeg Flowers

Foreword

When you do something you love you never work a day in your life! This holds true for me since I have in the past enjoyed very much writing for children. Sharing my stories came easy to me as I was a parent myself. Later, I found myself loving other projects such as painting and sculpting. One day my family moved to the Nutmeg state.... Connecticut! I was then faced with an empty canvas that swept me off my feet; an empty garden beckoning to come alive!

As I ventured into this new found love; the gardening world, I came across the idea of starting containers in my garden. Though many may seem overwhelmed to set out to build an entire garden, I find that container gardening is easy and so much fun. Once your flowers bloom you can place them anywhere in your garden. Like an artist you control the color palette. I also enjoy planting straight into the garden grounds, dancing my fingers into the rich soil and finding ways to feed the garden so that it may give me a spectacular show in spring! Gardening has now become my true love! I have enjoyed learning about the different flowers that bloom throughout the year. I also have come to learn that I do not like all flowers, but I do like that all flowers seem to have their own personality.

Yes, it is true that it has taken me over a year to document information on flowers and plants in my garden. I must add that this experience has fostered in me a new sense of gratitude for the creator of all things. I hope that you the reader sense that same feeling as you go through the pages of my very first book on gardening.

Rosie Maisonave

TABLE OF CONTENTS

NUTMEG
FLOWERS

GARDENING IS ONE OF THE SINGLE MOST THERAPEUTIC METHODS TO RELEASE STRESS. ONE MUST REMEMBER HOWEVER, WITHOUT THE PROPER EQUIPMENT UNDER A HOT SUN IT CAN ROB YOU FROM THE JOY OF GARDENING. LETS AVOID TURNING THIS AMAZING LEISURE INTO AN ARDUOUS ONE. LETS BE SAFE AND ENJOY THE GARDENING EXPERIENCE!

FIRST STEP: LETS GET THE BEST AND THE MOST COMFORTABLE LOOSE CLOTHING POSSIBLE. COVERING YOUR ARMS FROM THE SUN WITH A COMFY SHIRT IS A WAY TO GO. DON'T FORGET SHOES THAT ALLOW COMFORT FOR LONG STANDING AND GRIP FOR STEPPING ONTO HARD OR MUDDY SURFACES. SECOND STEP: A GREAT SUN BLOCK A PAIR OF SHADES AND THE RIGHT HEAD COVER WILL ALLOW THE RELEASE OF STRESS WITH NO INTERRUPTIONS!

READY, SET, LET'S GO GARDENING!

SPRING TIME

Spring time always brings in a hurried spray of colorful flowers such as tulips, hyacinths, daffodils, dahlias, magnolias, hydrangea to name of few and oh! My all time favorite the wide variety of the peony flower. I can honestly say that i only have experience with a few of these magnificent blooms. I hope the following pages tell the story of my fun filled passion for flowers, and like me you too can experience the joy of gardening!

MY LOVE FOR FLOWERS STARTED SPRING OF 2022 WITH THE EASIEST: TULIP BULBS.

WITH PLENTY OF RESEARCH I DECIDED THAT MY SMALL GARDEN NEEDED A WOW FACTOR... THEREFORE I DECIDED TO PLANT AKEBONO TULIP BULBS!

THE AKEBONO TULIP GROWS 24 INCHES SHINING A SPECTACULAR SOFT BUTTERY YELLOW AND A PIN RED STRIPE LINE DOWN ITS EDGES. AN ABSOLUTELY MUST HAVE IN YOUR GARDEN. THEY ALSO MAKE AMAZING CUTTING FLOWERS AS THEY ADD LUXURY TO ANY FLOWER ARRANGEMENT.

AKEBONO TULIP

THE AKEBONO TULIP
GREETED ME EVERY
MORNING UNDER THE
SPRING SUN AS IT DANCED
ABOVE THE BOX WOOD
GREENERY AROUND THEM.

WHETHER YOU'RE PLANTING
THEM IN YOUR GARDEN
OR STRAIGHT INTO A
CONTAINER ...WITH THE
PROPER CARE...MAKING
SURE THEY ARE HAPPILY
GROWING IN THEIR
CORRECT ENVIRONMENT, ITS
GUARANTEED THAT YOU'LL
END UP WITH THE MOST
BEAUTIFUL FLOWERS WITH
TOTAL BRAGGING RIGHTS
OVER THEM!

AT FULL BLOOM THEY ARE
TRULY AN EYE STOPPER.
ALTHOUGH THEY START
LOOKING LIKE A COMMON
BUDDED TULIP, THEY WILL
BLOSSOM LUXURIOUS HEALTHY
LAYERED PETALS. TRULY
MAKING THEM SEEM AS IF THEY
ARE THE 'QUEEN' AMONGST
THE COMMON TULIP.

NOTE:
FOR MORE INFORMATION
ABOUT PLANTING BULBS IN
EARLY FALL PLEASE SEE SECTION
OF THIS BOOK ON PLANTING
BULBS IN CONTAINERS.

THERE ARE MANY VARIETIES OF THE MAGNOLIA TREE, IN FACT AS OF 2020 THERE HAVE BEEN OVER 200 DOCUMENTED! EACH GIVING ITS COLORFULLY SHAPED PETALED FLOWER. IN THE NUTMEG STATE OF CONNECTICUT, THE MORE COMMONLY KNOWN ONE IS THE MAGNOLIA TREE CALLED THE 'SUNSATION'. MY HUSBAND AND I HAVE GROWN UNBEKNOWN TO US A 'SUNSATION' MAGNOLIA TREE. WHAT WE THOUGHT TO BE A FOUR-FOOT PLANT, WHICH HAD FOUR MATURE MAGNOLIAS ON IT, HAS GROWN INTO A 10 FOOT TREE! I LATER LEARNED THAT THIS VARIETY BLOOMS HUNDREDS OF MAGNOLIAS SUCH AS IT DID THIS YEAR.

ONCE FLOWER STARTS ITS BLOOM STAGE IT QUICKLY GROWS INTO ITS MATURE WIDTH OF 7" WIDE. A SUNSATION MAGNOLIA TREE CAN REACH ABOUT 20 - 30 FEET! ITS FLOWERS BLOOM EARLY TO MID-SPRING AND HAPPILY CAN GROW IN FULL SUN TO PARTIAL SHADE.

MAGNOLIA SUNSATION

THE MAGNOLIA STELLATTA 'ROYAL STAR' FLOWER NAME WHICH IS REFERRING TO ITS STAR-LIKE SHAPE FLOWERS.

BEST GROWN IN MOIST, ORGANICALLY RICH, WELL-DRAINED SOIL WILL NOT TOLERATE DRY SOIL. LOVES THE MOISTURE THAT COMES WITH HOT SUMMER DAYS. THE STELLATTA 'ROYAL STAR' GROWS BEST IN AREAS THAT PROTECTS IT FROM HIGH WINDS. WHEN IT COMES TO USING MULCH (I PREFER COMPOST OR PINE BARK MULCH), IT HELPS RETAIN SOIL MOISTURE. ONLY PRUNE IF NEEDED, PREFERABLY RIGHT AFTER FLOWERING.

THE STELLATTA IS NATIVE TO JAPAN. IT IS A SMALL TREE THAT CAN GROW UP TO 15-20' TALL. IT IS ALSO OFTEN GROWN AS A LARGE ROUNDED SHRUB. IT IS NOTED FOR ITS COMPACT SIZE AND ITS BEAUTIFUL CREAMY WHITE STAR SHAPED FLOWERS.

FULLY BLOOMED STELLATTAS IN EARLY SPRING. PHOTO DEMONSTRATES STELLATTAS GROWING AS A BEAUTIFUL WIDE HEDGE. NO GREENERY.

PHOTO DEMONSTRATES A LUSH GREEN WIDE HEDGE AFTER STAR SHAPED FLOWERS HAVE DIED OFF. THIS LUSH GREENERY WILL LAST THROUGHOUT THE SUMMER DAYS

MAGNOLIA
STELLATTA
'ROYAL STAR'

THERE ARE AT LEAST 40 DIFFERENT TYPES OF PEONY THAT GROW NATURALLY IN THE WILD; THAT NUMBER IS STILL BEING DISPUTED AMONGST THE BOTANISTS. THE GARDENIA PEONY (PAEONIA LACTIFLORA GARDENIA PEONY) WILL FLOWER FOR 7-10 DAYS. THIS IS ONE OF TWO TYPES OF PEONIES I HAVE IN MY GARDEN. THE GARDENIA IS AN EARLY MID AND LATE BLOOMING VARIETY. THE DOUBLE FLOWERS OPEN FROM SOFT PINK BUDS INTO 8-10 INCHES IN WIDTH. LUXURIOUSLY SHAPED CREAMY WHITE WITH A VERY LIGHT BLUSH AND GOLDEN STAMENS. THEY TEND TO HAVE RELIABLE AND VIGOROUS LEAVES THAT LAST THROUGHOUT THE SUMMER UNTIL FROST AND OFTEN COLORS UP IN THE FALL. THEY ENJOY FULL SUN TO PART SHADE.

1-

2-

3-   -4

IF YOU ARE GROWING THEM OUTSIDE NO WORRIES THEY ARE VIRTUALLY PEST FREE. THEY ARE LOW MAINTENANCE FLOWER. ITS NICE TO KNOW THAT THEY ARE ATTRACTIVE TO BUTTERFLIES! NOW ONCE FLOWER FADES CUT BACK PLANT AFTER THE FOLIAGE HAS DIED DOWN. WITH A LOT OF LOVE THIS VARIETY WILL FLOWER YEAR AFTER YEAR AS SOME CAN LAST UP TO FIFTY YEARS!

LONG LIVE THE PEONY!

1. SECOND WEEK OF APRIL COMMENCEMENT OF STEM GROWTH. AFTER REACHING FOUR FEET HIGH BUDS BEGIN TO APPEAR.
2. LAST WEEK OF MAY BUDS ARE LARGER IN SIZE EXPOSING COLOR OF FLOWER.
3. PETALS START PEELING BACK IN SOME OTHERS OPEN UP IN CIRCULAR SHAPE EXPOSING THE CREAMY INNER FLOWER.
4. AT THIS STAGE ONE CAN SEE THAT THIS FLOWER IS READY TO EXPLODE OPEN AND IT DID... ON THE FIRST DAY OF JUNE. (FULL BLOOM OPPOSITE PAGE).

GARDENIA PEONY
PAEONIA LACTIFLORA 'GARDENIA' (PEONY)

THE FESTIVA MAXIMA HAS MILKY PETALS AND ARE EDGED WITH RIPPLES OF COLORS THAT SOME CALL RASPBERRY. DEFINITE GORGEOUS BLOOMS EACH IS A PERFECT WORK OF ART! EACH LOVELY FLOWER BLOOMS 8" AND SMELLS AMAZING! MAKES AN ABSOLUTELY BEAUTIFUL ARRANGEMENT OF CUT FLOWERS. ONE WILL HAVE TO STAKE THEM AS BLOOMS TEND TO BEND OVER EACH OTHER. THEY GROW AFTER ALL UP TO 3 FEET.

THOUGH THEY MAKE GREAT CUTTING FLOWERS ONCE CUT THEY WILL DEPEND ON YOU TO FRESHEN THEM UP EVERYDAY WITH COLDWATER...ADD ICE IF YOU MUST... THEY WILL LAST LONGER. I'VE LEARN THAT I CAN'T KEEP THEM FOREVER BUT, THEY DO COME BACK YEAR AFTER YEAR. I MUST ADD THAT I ABSOLUTELY LOVE THEIR AMAZING FRAGRANCE IT FILLS UP A ROOM. REMEMBER HAVE FUN WITH THEM THEY ARE KNOWN TO BE WITHIN THE LUXURY LINE OF THE PEONY FLOWER.

THE FESTIVA MAXIMA

I RECEIVED TWO PHOTOS OF DIFFERENT PEONIES WHICH I HAVE NO EXPERIENCE WITH. THEIR VIBRANT COLORS ARE SPECTACULAR. SINCE I DO NOT HAVE EXPERIENCE WITH THEM I HAD TO DO A LITTLE RESEARCH. THE FOLLOWING IS A SMALL COLLECTION OF INFORMATION ON EACH FLOWER.

PHOTOGRAPHY BY: DENISSE SAAVEDRA

THE DR. ALEXANDER FLEMING PEONY. IN MY RESEARCH I LEARNED THAT THIS PEONY'S DESIGN IS COMPARED TO A CAN CAN DANCER'S PETTICOAT AND ITS FRAGANT, CALLED SUGAR-PINK CONFECTION WHOA! IT BLOOMS 8" IN WIDTH AS ITS STEMS GROW A LITTLE OVER 3 FEET. ITS NICE TO NOTE THAT THEY PRODUCE EXTRAVAGANT ARRANGEMENTS THAT PERFUME THE AIR!

DR. ALEXANDER FLEMING

THE BOWL OF BEAUTY
PEONY IS A JAPANESE
FLOWER. IT BLOOMS
PRETTY MAUVE PINK
PETALS. THEY HAVE A
LIGHT SWEET SCENT
AND CAN ADORN
THE GARDEN WITH
ITS FLUFFY RUFFLE
OF CREAM STAMENS.
FLOWER GROWS 8" IN
WIDTH AS ITS STEMS
GROW 3 FEET. MOST
PEONIES NEED A
STAKING BUT DUE TO
THEIR STRONG STEMS
THE BOWL OF BEAUTY
MAY NOT NEED THE
SUPPORT.

BOWL OF BEAUTY PEONY

CONTAINER GARDENING
CAN BE EASY AND FUN TO
COLOR YOUR GARDEN. COME
THE EARLY DAYS OF SPRING
WITH ITS READY TO DISPLAY
BUDDED FILLED CONTAINERS,
YOU MAY WANT TO START
THINKING OF BRINGING
THESE BEAUTIES INDOORS
AS SOON AS THEY BLOOM.

FOX TROT TULIPS

THESE BEAUTIES BECOME
CUTTING FLOWERS
THAT CAN BE USED FOR
SO MANY OCCASIONS.
WHETHER IT'S FOR
PLACING THEM INTO
A VASE, OR USED FOR
A WEDDING, PERHAPS
AS AN ANNIVERSARY
GIFT, OR YOU WANT TO
DRESS UP YOUR DINNER
TABLE. YOU WILL HAVE
SO MUCH TO CHOOSE
FROM AND PLENTY
OF DESIGN OPTIONS.

LILAC WONDER

RANUNCULUS MIX

AKEBONO TULIP

PEONY TULIP

GRAPE HYACINTHS

DIDIER TULIP

NARCISSUS DAFFOFIL AND
ART DESIGN DAFFODIL

ART DESIGN DAFFODIL

ANEMONE WINDFLOWER

COLORFUL BLOOMS DANCING WITHIN YOUR GARDEN IN CONTAINERS UNDER A GLOWING WARM SUN TRULY INVITES THE DESIGNER IN YOU TO CREATE A BEAUTIFUL ARRANGEMENT.

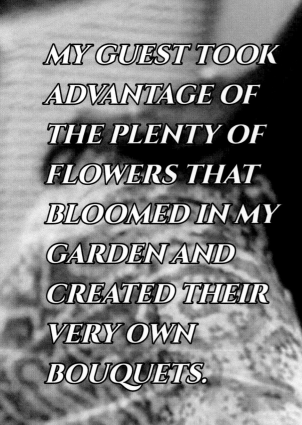

MY GUEST TOOK ADVANTAGE OF THE PLENTY OF FLOWERS THAT BLOOMED IN MY GARDEN AND CREATED THEIR VERY OWN BOUQUETS.

I FOUND THAT MY GUEST LOVE TO PLAY WITHIN THE SANDBOX OF FLOWERS. THE JOY OF GARDENING ALMOST RUBS OFF ON THEM. IT SEEMS THEY WERE THE HAPPIEST AS THE WERE ABLE TO CUT AND ARRANGE THEIR OWN FLOWERS INTO A SPRINGY BOUQUET. FOLLOWED BY A SILKY COLORFUL RIBBON TO TIE THEIR BUNDLE OF FLOWERS, HELPED THEM TO APPRECIATE ALL THE HARD LOVING WORK THAT WAS PUT INTO GROWING THEM.

I WANTED TO GO A STEP FURTHER WITH MY BLOOMS SINCE THEY WILL NOT BE COLORING MY GARDEN FOR VERY LONG. I DECIDED TO GATHER SEVERAL OF MY BLOOMS AND USE THEM TO BEAUTIFY MY TABLE FOR A GARDENING TEA PARTY! I PERSONALLY DECIDED TO PICK A LUXURIOUS SELECTION OF FLOWERS AND DID NOT SHY AWAY FROM USING VIBRANT COLORS. THE FLOWERS EFFORTLESSLY DRESSED UP MY PLATES AND TABLE AS THEIR FRAGRANCE FILLED THE AIR. IT MADE FOR A DEFINITE WOW! FACTOR.

TABLE DRESSED IN 'SUNSATION MAGNOLIAS',
'MIXED RANUNCULUS', 'DAFFODILS', AND
'PEONY TULIPS'

GATHERING THE PALETTE OF COLOR WAS SO
MUCH FUN FOR MY GUEST IT MADE FOR AN
UNFORGETTABLE TEA PARTY.

BOUQUET GATHERING AND TEA PARTY PHOTOS BY:
JOSH LIBATIQUE

WITH HUNDREDS OF IDEAS ON HOW AND WHAT TO PLANT
ON THE INTERNET, I TOOK TO THE DAHLIA FLOWER. ITS
AMAZING TO LEARN THAT THE HISTORY OF THE DAHLIA
FLOWER FAMILY TAKES YOU BACK TO THE YEAR OF 1525
WHEN THE CONQUISTADORS ARRIVED IN MEXICO AND
CENTRAL AMERICA.

IN OUR PRESENT DAY THESE BEAUTIFUL BLOOMS CONTINUE
TO DRAW SERIOUS INTEREST. THE HORTICULTURAL
CULTIVATION OF THE DAHLIA PLANT HAS RESULTED IN
OVER 57,000 CULTIVARS ...WHOA!

THE VAST VARIETIES OF DAHLIAS ARE REGISTERED,
AND PRESENTLY THESE BEAUTIES ARE LISTED IN THE
INTERNATIONAL REGISTER OF DAHLIA NAMES.

WITH SO MUCH INTEREST DRAWN IN THE VAST VARIETY
OF THESE FLOWERS, THEY HAVE BECOME TO GARDENERS A
SERIOUS BREED OF BLOOMS.

CONTAINER GARDENING WITH DAHLIAS

I HAVE LEARNED SO MUCH OF THESE AMAZING FLOWERS. I BEGAN EXPERIMENTING WITH THE "DINNER PLATE CAFE AU LAIT DAHLIA" AND A MIX OF CAFE AU LAIT DAHLIAS CALLED "THE DINNER PLATE CAFE AU LAIT COLLECTION OF DAHLIAS". BOTH OF WHICH I STARTED MY CONTAINER GARDENING.

I HAD SO MUCH FUN WATCHING THESE AMAZING FLOWERS GROW AND SHARING MY EXPERIENCE WITH FRIENDS. I DOCUMENTED IN WRITING AND TOOK PLENTY OF PHOTOS. MEASURING EACH AS THEY BEGAN TO GROW IN THEIR CONTAINERS HELPED ADD TO MY LEARNING OF THESE BEAUTIFUL FLOWERS.

USING THE PROPER FERTILIZER HELPED ME NOURISH THESE BABIES AS THEY ARE BOTH HUNGRY AND THIRSTY BLOOMS.

I HOPE YOU, THE READER, CAN FIND THIS SECTION EXCITING ENOUGH TO START PLANTING YOUR OWN DAHLIAS, AND SEE THE WONDER OF THIS MAGNIFICENT BLOOM!

CAFE AU LAIT DAHLIA

THE CAFE AU LAIT DAHLIA IS A TALL PLANT AND WILL NEED A STAKING SYSTEM AS WEIGHT OF FLOWER WILL BEND OVER LONG STEMS.

PLACE STAKING SYSTEM AFTER YOU PLANT DAHLIA PODS AND/OR SEEDS. LATER LARGE LEAVES WILL NOT ALLOW A PROPER STAKING. THIS STEP SHOULD BE DONE IMMEDIATELY AFTER PLANTING. YOU WILL NOT REGRET IT!

THE CAFE AU LAIT DAHLIAS ARE GOOD FOR CREATING HEIGHT IN ANY ARRANGEMENT. WITH SO MANY TO CHOOSE FROM THE CAFE AU LAIT DAHLIA LENDS ITSELF TO DISPLAY ELEGANCE IN YOUR ARRANGEMENTS.

12 DAYS ALREADY OVER 2 INCHES HIGH

2 MONTHS 3 1/2 FEET SHOWING FLOWER BUD

ABOVE PHOTO SHOWS 3 1/2 FEET TALL BUDDED
FLOWERS WITH LIMPED LEAVES UNDER A
SWELTERING HOT PRELONGED FULL SUNLIGHT

ABOVE PHOTO SHOWS 3 1/2 FEET TALL BUDDED
FLOWERS WITH PERKY HEALTHY GREEN LEAVES
UNDER A PARTIAL TO FULL SUNLIGHT.

THE CAFE AU LAIT DAHLIA GROWS 48" AND THIS BLOOM WILL LAST
JUNE THROUGH THE FROST. FLOWER REQUIRES PLENTY OF SUN.
HOWEVER FOR BEST RESULTS FULL MORNING SUN ONLY. IF YOU ARE
GROWING FLOWERS WITHIN A GARDEN BED TRY TO AVOID ALL DAY
FULL SUNLIGHT BY SHADING YOUR FLOWER BED AND/OR CONTAINER.

*NOTE: YOU CAN MOVE IT MUCH EASIER OUT OF THE HOT SUN IF
GROWING IN A CONTAINER A METHOD I PREFER.*

1 INCH

**BOOMED BLOOM!
8 INCHES ROUND ...WOW!**

8 INCHES

ISN'T SHE LOVELY?

A FEW NOTES.....

I WAS DEFINITELY SUCCESSFUL WITH MY DINNER PLATE CAFE AU LAIT DAHLIAS! HOWEVER, NOT SO SUCCESSFUL WITH THE MIX DAHLIAS. IT SEEMS AS A LEARNING FOR ME THAT EACH DAHLIA PREFERS A CERTAIN CARE. THE DINNER PLATE 8-10 INCH GROWTH DAHLIAS PREFER LESS SUN AS TO THE MIX PREFER LOTS OF SUN. THEY ARE BOTH HUNGRY BLOOMS AND REQUIRE PLENTY OF WATER. SOMEHOW TREATING THEM THE SAME I LOST ALONG THE WAY THE GROWING PROCESS FOR THE MIX DAHLIAS. SOME BLOOMED AND WERE NOT AS HEALTHY IT SADDENS ME THAT MY GREEN THUMB FAILED! UGH! BUT NEVERTHELESS I TRULY ENJOYED THE PROCESS.

MIXED DINNER PLATE
CAFE AU LAIT DAHLIA

3 DAYS AFTER PLANTING!

60 DAYS AFTER PLANTING THE MIXED
DINNER PLATE SHOWS DIFFERENT HEIGHTS
OF THE MIXED DAHLIAS ABOUT TO BLOOM

NATURAL BLOOMING PROCESS FOR THE MIXED
DINNER PLATE CAFE AU LAIT DAHLIAS

UNHEALTHY BLOOM PURPLE DAHLIA NEVER
FINISH SHOWING ALL ITS POTENTIAL PETALS.

THE GENUS HYDRANGEA

THE HYDRANGEA IS A SHRUB WITH ROUNDED OR FLATTENED FLOWERING HEAD OF SMALL FLORETS, THE OUTER ONES OF WHICH ARE TYPICALLY INFERTILE. HYDRANGEAS ARE NATIVE TO ASIA AND AMERICA.

GENUS HYDRANGEA AN ORNAMENTAL SHRUB THAT BLOOMS IN LATE SUMMER AND ITS BIG-LEAF ARE COMMONLY GROWN IN GARDENS AND USED AS INDOOR HOUSE PLANTS.

I FIND THIS FLOWER TO MAKE EXCELLENT CUT FLOWERS AND AFTER THEY DRY THEY HOLD THEIR BEAUTY. IT'S HARD TO DISCARD THEM! WHEN WINTER ARRIVES THEIR DRIED FLORETS ARE STILL IN THEIR COLORFUL SPLENDOR.

THESE BEAUTIES GROW UP TO 10 FEET TALL SHRUB AND ALL.
HOWEVER, THERE ARE PLENTY OF VARIETIES THAT STAY MORE
COMPACT. HYDRANGEA FLORETS GROW UP TO 12 INCHES ACROSS
AND CAN REMAIN GORGEOUS FOR SEVERAL WEEKS.

HERE WE HAVE MY DEAR FRIEND
ISHA. A LOVER OF THESE BEAUTIFUL
BLOOMS. SHE IS SHOWING HOW
JUST A SINGLE BLOOM CAN BRING
ELEGANCE INTO YOUR SPACE.

HERE WE HAVE GINETTE MY SISTER,
MY FRIEND. SHE IS ANOTHER LOVER
OF THESE BEAUTIFUL BLOOMS! SHE IS
DISPLAYING THAT THIS GORGEOUS
HYDRANGEA, PICKED FROM MY
GARDEN, CAN POSSIBLY BE LARGER
THAN SOMEONES HEAD.... THIS PICK
BROUGHT HER JOY!

DISPLAYING DRIED UP HYDRANGEA AS THEY STILL HOLD-UP THEIR BEAUTY

LAST HYDRANGEA FROM MY
GARDEN. TO BE LEFT IN WATER
UNTIL WATER DRIES UP AND
FLORETS KEEP THEIR COLOR
AND GLORY. IT WILL DRESS-UP
MY KITCHEN THROUGHOUT
THE WINTER FOR SURE!

ANOTHER BEAUTIFUL SUMMER
BLOOM IS THE CRAPE MYRTLE.
GROWS IN LATE SUMMER AND
WHEN IN IT'S FULL BLOOM IT BECKONS
TO BE CUT AND PUT INTO A VASE!

THE CLUSTER OF
HOT PINK UNDER
THE SUN IS
BREATH TAKING!

CRAPE MYRTLE

CONTAINER FOLIAGE
AN ART OF GREENERY

BOUGAINVILLEA SPECTABILIS

DOROTHEANTHUS
(FLOWERED OPPOSITE PAGE)

VINCA MAJOR

CREEPING JENNY

A WIDE COLLECTION OF FOLIAGE CAN GIVE HOMAGE TO OUR GARDENS BIG OR SMALL, WHETHER THEIR MIXED INTO OUR OUTDOOR FLOWER POTS OR IN OUR HOMES.

MIX 'EM UP! HAVE FUN WITH YOUR OUTDOOR FOLIAGE. DRESS UP YOUR CERAMIC POTS AND CONTAINERS. THEY COME IN ALL SHAPES AND SIZES AND WILL LAST THROUGHOUT THE SPRING AND SUMMER SEASON!

(LEFT SIDE OF MAIN ENTRANCE)

FULL GROWTH
OF SMALL PLANTS
IN CONTAINERS.
CONTAINERS
PLACED RIGHT
AND LEFT SIDE
OF MAIN HOUSE
ENTRANCE.

I HAD TO TRIM
SEVERAL TIMES
AS THEY WERE
RECEIVING
EXCELLENT
SUNLIGHT
AND WATERED
EVERY DAY.

FRONT DOOR
CONTAINERS
CAN BE AN EYE
STOPPER WHEN
PROPERLY LOVED!

(RIGHT SIDE OF MAIN ENTRANCE)

THE HARDY MUMS

MOST FOLKS CONSIDER
SUMMER THE MOST COLORFUL
SEASON IN THE GARDEN, BUT
AUTUMN ISN'T SHY EITHER
ABOUT PUTTING ON A SHOW!

DURING THE DREARY COLD
LONG DAYS OF WINTER MANY
OF THE GARDENERS ARE
TIRED AND WORN OUT, AND
WELCOME THE COMING OF
SPRING WITH PERKY FLOWERS
THAT SAVE US FROM THE
WINTER BLUES SURE TO COME.

HOWEVER, GARDENERS ARE
JUST AS HAPPY IN THE EARLY
DAYS OF AUTUMN. THE AIR
STARTS TO FEEL DRYER LEAVING
BEHIND THE LONG MUGGY
DAYS OF LATE SUMMER. THE
LEAVES ARE FALLING ABOUT
THE GROUND AND YES, THANKS
TO OUR LOCAL SUPERMARKETS,
AND NURSERIES, WE CAN
GET OUR HANDS ON BOTH
LARGE AND SMALL COLORFUL
POTTED MUMS!

THEY ARE EVERYWHERE! DRESS
UP YOUR GARDEN THEY TRULY
INVITE YOU AND YOUR GUEST
TO SMILE!

THEIR COLORFUL BLOOMS
CAN BE A SHOW STOPPER
DURING THE COOL DAYS OF
FALL.

CHOOSING THE RIGHT SPOT
IN YOUR GARDEN WITH
AT LEAST SIX HOURS OF
SUN A DAY, A LITTLE LOVE,
AND YOUR GARDEN IS
FRESHENED UP!

THEY COME IN GLORIOUS
COLORS AND EACH WILL
DISPLAY THE BEAUTY THAT
COMES WITH THE CRISP
DAYS OF AUTUMN.

CONTAINER GARDENING

PLANTING YOUR BULBS
EARLY FALL

PLANTING BULBS IN CONTAINERS WITH HOPES OF A HEALTHY BLOOM IS ALL NEW TO ME. I BELIEVE ...WELL... I HOPE I'VE COLLECTED THE RIGHT AMOUNT OF FERTILIZER AND PROPER SOIL. WITH ALL MY BULBS IN POTS AND CAREFULLY STORED, I CAME TO REALIZE THIS FUN ADVENTURE MAY BRING PLENTY OF COLOR INTO MY GARDEN NEXT SPRING.

TAKE NOTE: BULBS SHOULD BE PLANTED NO SOONER THEN LATE OCTOBER TO NO LATER THEN EARLY NOVEMBER. YOU WOULD WANT ALL BULBS PLANTED IN SOIL BEFORE THE FROST COMES INTO YOUR AREA. CHECK YOUR ALMANAC AND FIND OUT WHEN IS THE FIRST DAY OF FROST IN YOUR AREA.

ALSO, TO MAKE THE WELCOMING OF EACH BLOOMED BULB EASIER TO IDENTIFY PLACE LABELS ON EACH POT WITH ITS NAME.

DURING THE PLANTING STAGE, ONE MAY FEEL THAT PLANTING EACH BULB CAN BE A LITTLE PAINSTAKING. THIS WILL BE THE MOMENT YOU REALIZE THAT GARDENING IS AN ABSOLUTE LABOR OF LOVE.

...READY, SET, LET'S GET THOSE BULBS IN THE CONTAINERS!

I STARTED WITH MY FAVORITE
AKEBONO TULIP BULBS

AFTER YOU PLACE BULBS IN SOIL LAYER FERTILIZED SOIL ON TOP AND WATER WITH PLENTY OF WATER.

AT THIS POINT WATER PLENTY AND COVER IF NECESSARY. BULBS MUST BE KEPT IN A COOL DRY DARK AREA SUCH AS YOUR GARAGE, THROUGHOUT THE WINTER MONTHS.

YOU HAVE TO BABY THEM AND MAKE SURE SOIL IS KEPT MOIST, NOT DRENCHED, THROUGHOUT WINTER.

KEEPING THEM AWAY FROM YOUR GARDEN IS ONE THING I PREFER BEFORE ITS TIME TO TAKE THEM OUT INTO THE GARDEN IN SPRING.

WHY? BECAUSE LAST YEAR THAT DARN CHIPMUNK ATE OVER 20 OF MY PLANTED BULBS!!! LESSON LEARNED!

I CONTINUED PLANTING MANY TYPES OF BULBS. I WILL DEMONSTRATE IN THE FOLLOWING PHOTOS THE VARIETY OF SIZES AND SHAPES OF THE BULBS IN ITS AMAZINGLY DESIGNED DORMANT STATE.

I USED PLASTIC POTS BOTH NEW AND OLD. (I ALWAYS SAVED POTS FROM PAST PURCHASED PLANTS). I STARTED THIS NEW ADVENTURE USING FORTY-TWO POTS IN TOTAL. WHOA!

IN THIS NEW GARDENING JOURNEY I PLANTED

NAMES OF THE PLANTED BULBS

AKEBONO TULIPS
DIDIER TULIPS
FOX TROT TULIPS
LILAC WONDER TULIPS
DAFFODIL NARCISSUS
DAFFODIL ART DESIGN
GRAPE HYACINTH (MUSCARI LATIFOLIUM)
PURPLE SENSATION (ALLIUM TYPE)
ANEMONE BLANDA MIX (WIND FLOWER)
CROCUS YELLOW

THE FOLLOWING BULBS ARE STILL IN A GROWTH PROCESS...
AS THEY ARE THREE OF THE MOST INTERESTING UNIQUELY
DESIGNED FLOWERS, I WILL INCLUDE THEM IN MY NEXT
BOOK ON GARDENING.

GLAMOUR UNIQUE
GIANT PEACH
VANILLA COUP

EACH BULB COMES WITH ITS
SPACING AND DEPTH PLANTING
INSTRUCTIONS. I HOWEVER CHOSE
TO NOT SPACE THEM OUT TOO FAR
FROM EACH OTHER AS THIS IS ALL
A TESTING GROUND FOR ME. LAST
YEAR I DID THE SAME WITH MY
AKEBONO TULIPS AROUND MY TREE
AND THEY GREW SPECTACULAR. BUT
IF YOU CHOOSE TO SPACE THEM
OUT ACCORDINGLY BY ALL MEANS
DO SO!

REMEMBER TO LABEL ALL YOUR POTS

FOR THE FIRST WATERING YOU MUST WATER
HEAVILY...COVER THEM THIS WILL HELP BULB
TO MAINTAIN DORMANT THROUGHOUT
THE WINTER MONTHS. YOU MUST MAINTAIN
THEM IN A DRY COLD DARK PLACE SUCH AS
YOUR GARAGE. TRY TO KEEP SOIL MOIST BY
WATERING THEM LIGHTLY ONCE A WEEK. IF
YOU FEEL THAT SOIL IS MOIST YOU SHOULD
WAIT UNTIL IT DRIES UP BEFORE WATERING
THEM AGAIN. TOO MUCH WATER CAN ROT
THE DORMANT BULB.

TRUE STORY: AS I PATIENTLY CARED FOR MY PLANTED BULBS DURING THE WINTER DAYS, TURNS OUT THAT UNBEKNOWN TO ME AND MANY OF THE GARDENERS THIS YEAR IN THE EASTERN REGION, UNEXPECTED WARM DAYS HAD CONTAINER PLANTED BULBS STRUGGLING TO STAY DORMANT. SINCE IT WAS NOT AN EXTREMELY STEADFAST COLD WINTER. THIS UNSEASONABLY WARM STRETCH CAUSED MANY OF THE BULBS TO PUSH THROUGH THE SOIL. I FOUND THAT MANY OF THE BULBS WERE COMMENCING A SPROUTING OF STEMS AND FORMING A GRASS LIKE PATCH IN THE CONTAINERS. I FELT A BIT DISHEARTENED AS I WANTED TO PREVENT THEIR GROWTH BEFORE THEIR TIME HOWEVER, THEIR IMPRESSIVE DESIGN PREVENTED GROWTH OF BUDS AND FLOWERING DURING WINTER DAYS. WHAT A RELIEF! THIS WOULD HAVE KILLED ALL MY FLOWERS AND THE JOY OF WAITING FOR THESE BEAUTIFUL BLOOMS WOULD HAVE UNFORTUNATELY COME TO AN UNTIMELY END!

THOUGH IT WAS TIME TO PLACE MY POTTED BULBS OUTDOORS, WE SURPRISINGLY RECEIVED ONE LAST BLAST OF WINTER. NEED NOT TO WORRY IF SUCH THING OCCURS, TURNS OUT THAT'S WATER STORED FOR THE DORMANT BULBS.

A NOTE TO THE READER:

...WELL I CANNOT BELIEVE AN ENTIRE YEAR AND A HALF HAS GONE BY. IT HAS BEEN WONDERFUL VENTURING IN MY GARDEN. AS MANY OF YOU GARDENERS KNOW WINTER IS FILLED WITH LONG COLD DAYS AND THE COLD GROUND HIDES ITS POTENTIAL LUSTER. DEPENDING ON HOW THE WEATHER PRESENTS ITSELF IN MARCH, SPRING CAN FEEL A WHOLE WORLD AWAY.

...YES, THE COLD STRETCHED DAYS AHEAD CAN ADD TO A LACK OF PATIENCE... BUT, DO NOT FRET... KEEP BUSY I LIKE TO DO PLENTY OF CUDDLING UP NEXT TO A WARM FIRE WITH FAMILY AND FRIENDS. IN MY HOME THERE IS ALWAYS THE AMAZING MULLING SPICES AND CINNAMON FLAVORS DANCING IN THE AIR. BACK IN MY SLEEPING GARDEN I FIND DRY TWIGS, ACORNS AND OTHER TWISTED BARE BRANCHES. I COLLECT THE BRANCHES JUST FOR FUN. I PLACE THEM IN A JAR JUST TO KEEP THOSE GARDENING JUICES FLOWING.

...COLLECTING DRY TWIGS FROM MY SLEEPING
GARDEN ADDS A LOVELY TOUCH OF WARM DECOR
TO THE INDOOR AMBIENCE.

...KEEPING THIS FRAME OF MIND IS PRETTY HELPFUL, AS I AWAIT FOR THE NEXT FLOWER SHOW MY GARDEN WILL DISPLAY.

...UNTIL THEN I'LL BE SEEING YOU IN YOUR GARDEN COME NEXT SPRING! FOR NOW, STAY WARM AND HEALTHY.

-ROSIE MAISONAVE

THANK YOU TO:

VICTORIA ACOSTA

GINETTE EALEY

ISHA FERNANDEZ

VANESSA LIBATIQUE

DENISSE SAAVEDRA

MY FRIENDS...

MY SISTERS...

WHO LOVE FLOWERS AS MUCH AS I DO.

TO THE READER...I HOPE THE PAGES OF THIS BOOK HAS FIRED UP THE GARDENER IN YOU!!

READY, SET, SEE YOU NEXT SPRING!

Printed in the United States
by Baker & Taylor Publisher Services